# Café after Dawn

Poems

Xiao Yan

Arcade Publishing • New York

This is not a diary.
This is a poetry

To my dear mom
She likes café
She doesn't like cat
She likes morning rather than dawn
She was so proud of me
And called me a goddess
She is immortal

There were two entrances to the café, but I always opted for the narrower one hidden in the shadows. I always chose the same table at the back of the little room and write my poems to you, day by day. Let the world around you fade. Get rid of your rolling cigarettes. Some beautiful things: warm nights after the rain, old books, tea in the afternoon, fresh laundry, and blurry moon. Yes, I'm writing this for you. This might justify your life.

**Genesis**

תא ,םיהלא ארב ,תישארב
.ץראה תאו ,םימשה

我看见你
世界就有光

When I see you
There is light

We took a deep breath
After you died
In the heart of summer
The morning full of storm

There was a galaxy in your eyes
Flames in your hands
Your tongue used to carry
rosemary and wine
Your skin so bright it burns my eyes

Chaos

The present determines the future
But the approximate present does not
Approximately determine the future

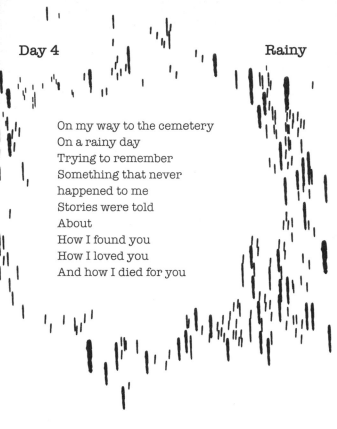

**Day 4**                                          **Rainy**

On my way to the cemetery
On a rainy day
Trying to remember
Something that never
happened to me
Stories were told
About
How I found you
How I loved you
And how I died for you

## Confession

To discover who I am
Imagine my soul departs from
my body
And I am face to face with
death
I know my body must be afraid
But I am not

In the woods I let him say
His words
They sounded
Like leaves
Years and years of leaves

So
it
begins to rain
In Damascus
Two years have passed
Since you
Came to my dream
Your silhouette appeared
In a film set in far-off lands
And that's enough for me to cry

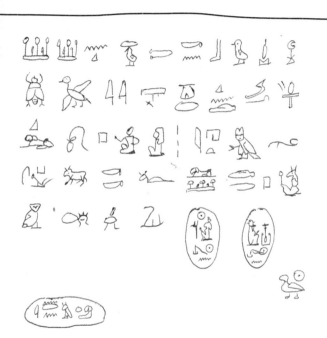

I let everyone go
People that I love
People that I hate
Then

I

am alone
Then I'm truly free

# Day 9                                    Blue

Love
Stay away from me
Just in case
I'm the poisoned one

In a room
Full of over-used furniture
I saw an attempted suicide
under my window

A setting sun
A broken leg
I saw what fear looked like in a
small face

Sin City

You asked me where to find Sin City
Said you needed a pilgrimage
I told you it is inside me
The ocean flowing into my lungs
Vaporized
The clouds flowing into my ears
Petrified
Tears become mountains
Woods become frost
Here, you hold the moon like a baptizer
And the sun dies when we breathe

I was a willow tree
Falling while standing

I was a battlefield
Fighting while breathing

I went to the desert
To look for truth
A camel trainer told me
He did not care about anything
Bigger than an atom
or smaller than the universe

A star
Passed away a thousand years
ago
Like our love
A fake flame

You once told me
In a language I could not read
In a dialect I had never heard
That I was never meant for you

You're in my words
Your voice, your warmth, and
your skin
So I write them down carefully
So I can read you again and
again


Forever

There are thousands of ways to
die
In this city
But I choose to die
In your embrace

In Paris,
In stone Cathedral,
A worm grows out
from an apple tree.

## Little Cat

Around three o'clock in the afternoon
Dim light
The sky was blue
palm trees were tall

I talked about wartime love affairs
With my little cat
And things we know that will fade away

My little cat
There was no winter as cold as her winter
There was no night as deep as her night

**Bella**

Bella was never as innocent
As others thought
Once she gave me a straight
gaze
It was a shred of order amid the
chaos
Through the ice, the heat, the
darkness, the fireworks
And the quarrels

John is a big boy
At the age of nineteen
I met him in Detroit
And it became a birthmark
That no one can touch

**Day 20**

Rose and mirror
Blood and crystal

## Day 21

My girlfriend was under the moon
She was drowned to death
I passed her by and noticed
There must be a bomb
Hidden inside her
And a silent volcano
Ignited by me somewhere in the
darkness

I was in a river
People burying me underneath
Stars falling like blood drops
Your lies were waterlilies
Then I saw the Taj Mahal burning
Worms growing out from evergreen
Your blue scarves flying in the wind
Stones burst like volcanos
Tears formed an iceberg
I was drowned and flown

A barking dog
The ripple of voices
The hush of the breeze
Chattering waves
Filling my nostrils and ears
I run
Outrun the wave
I have to learn
How to run far enough
inland
That the wave will never
Catch me

When the music f a d
I hear his whisper
In my ear
His voice has wings and asks me
To close my eyes and fly

My heart is a river
You sail away from it
without the fear of losing me
But when you return
I will still be there
Even if you're a thousand years late

**My best friend "Alexa"**

Late night in New York
After the pouring rain
In an empty space
Without a clue
Suddenly I said
"Alexa, play some music"
She played a weird song
Called Amo Soitanto Te
By Ed Sheeran
I said "Next one"
Oh, my best friend Alexa

Waiting for you
In the winter by the fireplace
With the food I bought for you
Whenever I'm with you
I feel bored
But I can never leave you
I feel your body
Your warmth
Your arms around me
I know deeply
That is a
Domestication

Never hold tight to anything

Staying at home all day
You feel a lot of things
Missing
Something must be
Missing
Every time when I see a sunset
Every time I finish a cup of
coffee
It always takes away something
From me
Which makes me feel sad

The dusty road is a straight
line to the horizon
In vain my emotions hide
between rocks
In the desert
I'm shouting

Take my sweet revenge
Through the mirror

Tonight some existentialists
Gathered together
And talked about the Second Sex
From Socrates to Plato
Hesse and carol

My mother gave me some advice:

Go to sleep

People are around
Living their lives
Selling vanilla ice cream
Making pancakes

What a wonderful world

# Day 33

"It sounds to me that they try
to kill you by changing your
way of existence."
"Yes, but no. I doubt
if I ever existed"

I was on the verge of waking up
It took me a long time getting ready
To exist, to feel, and to ignore
The mirror poisoned me
Tricked me into finding myself in it
Again and again
But all I saw
Was the surface of a postponed corpse
So I have to write
About bullets, mosquitos, flesh
And everything I failed to be
A truth that escaped from my dream
That we seek between hills and valleys

We have to write
To write is to forget
To be quiet with disquiet

She belongs to Rome, Mesopotamia
and Paris
You can find her in Eastern Europe
Taking a cross-border train
Or driving along the coast all day
You know she isn't real
She was a mere appearance
Dreamt by another
But the images she creates
Appear again and again

### Waltz

For that piano piece
I'm running away with him
To another century
With my soul and sin
Running into fire
I see the blue Mediterranean
So lost and yet so found

Strangers in the theatre
Buying aspirin
The night show never begins
So their backs suffer
We talk about the deaf and
blind
And are afraid of becoming
either
Before the cloud catches the
wind
Smoke gets in your eyes

**Day 38**

Speaking of power
If guns are yours
Words are mine

I happened to remember it all
My old house
The forest fire
The bullet you stole
The dust of the ring
The wedding full of saints and butterflies
The secret garden where the rose lays an egg
The church where people starve and survive
It's the end of the day
The moon is ready for bed

...

My life will be forgotten
So it will be forgiven?

**Day 41**                    **Breezy**


In the evening
Lovers embrace their tragedies
Hurry towards each other's
horizon
They miss old dreams
Of vague utopia
A place greater than deserts
With olive trees and hoarse voice
Windows open to the south


We cl<sup>i</sup>m<sup>b</sup> and     f
                        a

            l

        l

            Finally come back to the cradle

Pouring water
A lone child
Standing at a staircase made of light
So close to the moon
He brings me to a door
Which I cannot open
So we walk
And glare at each other in silence
We live together on a farm
Growing peaches and wounds
A lone child
Picking stars like pebbles

I remember nightfall
In the valley of the m⬤on
A wolf howls
You stab me in the back
I remember that blade
So pale yet so
                    **bright**

## AI Shakespeare

Alex is an AI scientist. One day, I was drinking
cappuccino in the cafe, he sent me this poem
written by a Shakespeare machine.

"Write the beginning of your poem, the
Shakespeare machine will complete it."
He wrote "when in the chronicle of wasted time"

**Here is the poem:**

When in the chronicle of wasted time
Bot than thy him have from my filtiin me thought,
As thee, that nof my live ey self-of thy foes,
Sabmed devery bound andy danse my môme,
Which for their proveses of levesy of my ston,
Which hall besued my love, his goddess nabe,
And for the worlt, and beaution wo my might.
That thee when i aver thy sum i saved my hall,
While curt encounter for me, afour wat haïrsed,
Save i noyau have sweet theers th

A poem

I hear
silence

Make huge **noise**
I scream as loud as I can
But no one hears

Sakura blooms
Snow falls
Your hair grows grey
And falls like a willow
A teardrop drops on a lotus leaf
An ice cube jumps into a volcano

**A sugar**
**cube**

*jumps* into the

Americano

It was my fault
For making her understand
What is hopelessness
And desperation
When she knows that
Flowers won't bloom again
And her children won't make children

I'm so tired of your
Poetic justice
Don't blame it on evil
We don't blame it on storm

Baby, can you get me out of this life?
I want it better
In another way
Another city
Another sun
A place where we don't belong

Day 50                          Calm


Gunfire


**Battles** on the streets **every day**
Stop reading news so
we won't be **afraid**

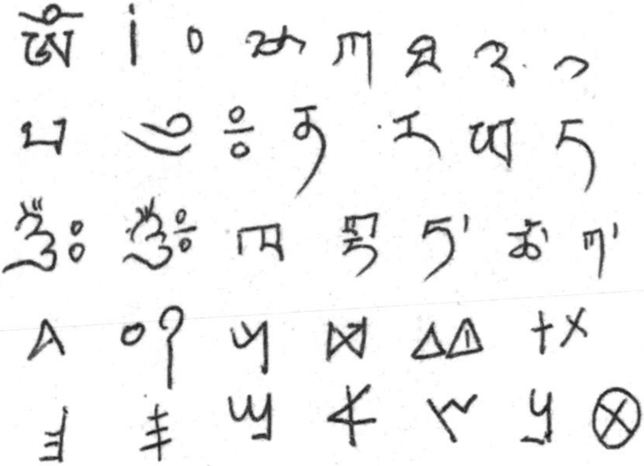

Saturday night
I took a secret trip to London
I miss her elegant word choice
And her sluggish way of finishing up a cup of coffee
I have never known a field
As wide as her mind
As wild as her dream

Atlantides

There was a ship
Returned to something older
Dawn appears upon the sea
Troops fade, the flowers remain

I'm going to the deep river
For a full moon, a white light
My lip touches yours before you evaporate

## WABI SABI

Things evolve from nothingness
Earthy, murky, simple
Rustic soul against electric sound
On the twilt shore
A single fisherman's hut
No one in town

To settle
To learn
To survive and prosper
To abandon and murder
Is it all for a better life?

It's reasonable to argue with
Alternative facts
When we live in alternative realities

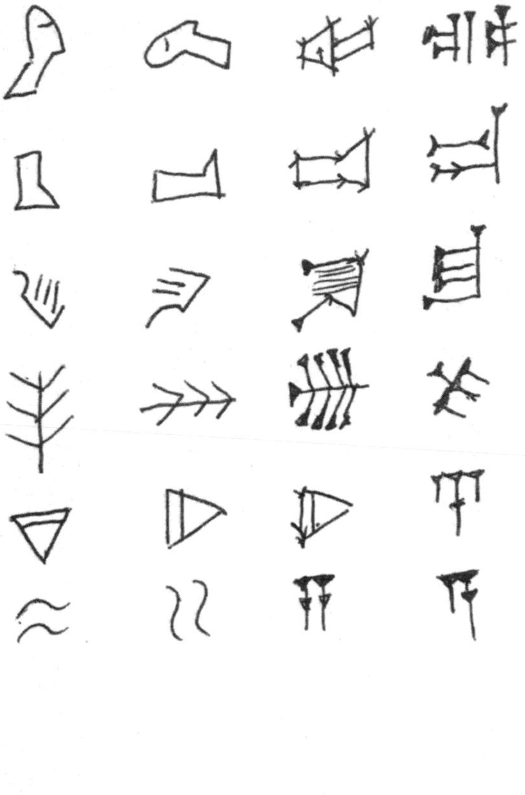

It's so cold outside the uterus
I'm just a little girl
Tired of drinking water
Missing that breast milk

Two young girls talking:

"She charged me four dollars on Venmo
Cause I used her paper towels
I'm not buying shit from her apartment"

"You should move out"


Tw**OO**ld men talking:

"That man lives in an apartment
Smaller than mine
Worth four million dollars!
That's crazy, just for the manhattan view."

"I rather live in a house in New Jersey."

There is no new thing upon the earth
"All knowledge is but memory
All novelty is but oblivion"
God had him die
And then revived him

So I repeat my mistakes

mɪstakes

Loneliness kills people,
Too smart, too stupid, too beautiful, too ugly
Anything beyond mediocre
Makes

you

alone

You continue to become her
Who never remembered your name
Every morning a rose rots in somebody's coffin
And you continue to grow
Inch by inch
The world gives you more and more things
That you don't need
And takes away everything you owned
You realize that little by little

Today I open my eyes without you
Cannot utter a word
So I stop trying

Let the light behind the shutters shine through
Let the crowd in the streets cry out
Let air form into a shape and come to me

I was born into a world full of animals wearing clothes
So I go naked

I was born into a world of color and sound
So I turn my TV into black & white and silence

I was born into a world people grabbing everything
As much as they can
So I learn to embrace the art of letting go

Look what you found
Life is easier without me
All the roads I took were detours
All the laughs I had were jokes
When I was older
All I did was to live and die
Crash and fly
No one is going to save us
Little cravings and desires
In my blood
Sink under an iceberg

Mother
Tell me
I am good
Tell me you're proud of me

Once you told me that you're the only one
Who loves me so much
In this lonely world
That when you're gone
There will be no other one
Who loves me like you do

I agree

So, Mother
Tell me I'm a good baby
Tell me
You're proud

# An Extra Day                    Bright

To finish this poetry
To justify You
And justify Me
For secret relief
I need a nap for another year

**Praise for *Café after Dawn***

"Xiao Yan's writing lives in the liminal spaces between utterance and silence, poetry and prose, quotidian and sacred. With a restlessly questioning mind, she negotiates the boundaries between ancient and modern, often finding--as interesting writing often does—that they can exist at once." —Joseph Fasano, poet of *Vincent, Inheritance*, and *Fugue for Other Hands*

"I have found Xiao Yan to be a widely multi-talented artist. Her artistic nature is completely integrated into her personality, and her perceptiveness flows into her work as a poet, visual artist, and singer. These poems filter her impressions of the life and death of her beautiful mother as it happened in recent years, as well as her experiences as a young woman with complicated feelings in a contradictory world. Her personal poetic language (here English is a second language where every word is savored and has a charged significance) encompasses indirect images that mingle with forthright truths plainly spoken, seriousness with sudden shifts of humor. She is sly, knowing, and naively pure in her very individual outlook." —Jane McMahan, voice professor at Barnard College, Columbia University

"A glistening dewdrop of a book." —Tad Crawford, author of *A Floating Life*

Arcade Publishing books may be purchased in bulk at special discounts
for sales promotion, corporate gifts, fund-raising, or educational purposes.
Special editions can also be created to specifications. For details, contact
the Special Sales Department, Arcade Publishing, 307 West 36th Street,
11th Floor, New York, NY 10018 or arcade@skyhorsepublishing.com.

Arcade Publishing® is a registered trademark of Skyhorse Publishing, Inc.®,
a Delaware corporation.

Visit our website at www.arcadepub.com.

10 9 8 7 6 5 4 3 2 1

Library of Congress Cataloging-in-Publication Data is available on file.

Cover design by Erin Seaward-Hiatt
Interior design by Chengyu Liu
Photos by Ye Fan

Print ISBN: 978-1-951627-05-8
Ebook ISBN: 978-1-951627-06-5

Printed in China